The Lost Key
at Peck's Cove

Uh-oh! Dad lost the key to the shed! He can't do his work without his tools. Scott and Jon want to help him find the key, but they find much more than that when they search the marshes and creeks at Peck's Cove.

ORIGINAL PUBLIC

The Good AND THE Beautiful
goodandbeautiful.com

ISBN 978-1-95292(

9 781952 920745

SKU 102

The Lost Key at Peck's Cove

By Amanda Parris

Illustrated by Nanette Regan

Cover illustration by Nanette Regan

Cover design by Anna Asfour

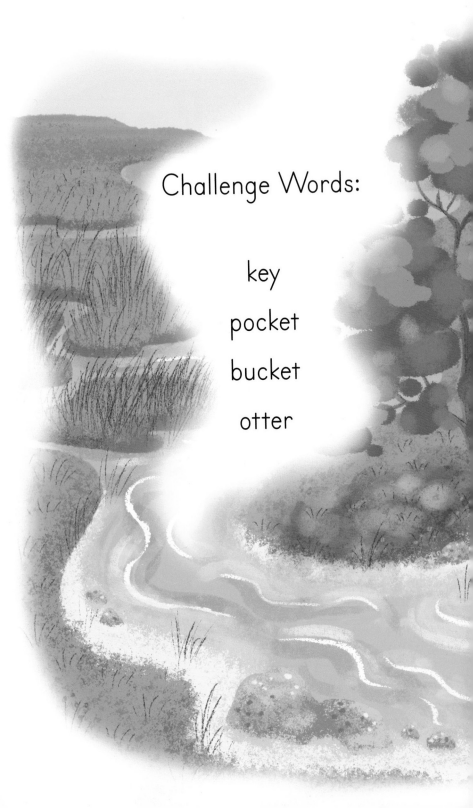

Challenge Words:

key

pocket

bucket

otter

The Gills had a home by the
marsh at Peck's Cove.

Bob Gill fixed cars for his job.

Kate Gill was a cook
and took care of the
boys, Scott and Jon.

Dad, Mom, Scott, and Jon all had jobs—big
and small—on the land by Peck's Cove.

The sun was hot one day as Scott
and Jon swam in the creek. Mom
called them for lunch.

Dad was in the shed. He
used his tools to try to fix
a car for Jim Brown.

Dad locked the shed and set the key in his pocket. He came in for lunch.

"Let's check our crab pots,"
Dad said when lunch was done.

A crab pot is a trap to catch crabs.
This was a job Scott and Jon shared.

After lunch the three went to the
marsh to check the traps.

9

The marsh smelled like salt and
mud. Bugs buzzed on grass stems
and in the sky.

A duck sat in the
grass. It poked its
bill down for a fish.

Dad took the line from each trap to check for crabs. Scott and Jon held the bucket.

"Five crabs for Mom to cook for us,"
said Dad with a smile.

Scott and Jon took the
bucket to Mom and went
back to the creek.

With bare feet
they chased small
fish to the sand.

15

Dad came to ask them, "Did you see my key? I lost the key to the shed."

Did it fall from his pocket?
Scott and Jon helped him look.

They checked by the shed ...

on the ground ...

and in the house.

At the marsh, they looked by the traps.

No key was found.

The next day, Dad was not able to get in the shed to use his tools.

He said, "I must get that key. I cannot use my tools if they are locked in the shed."

21

Scott and Jon tried to help
Dad. They went back to the
marsh to look.

Jon saw a blue
fly, but no key.

He looked at big fluffy
clouds in the sky.

23

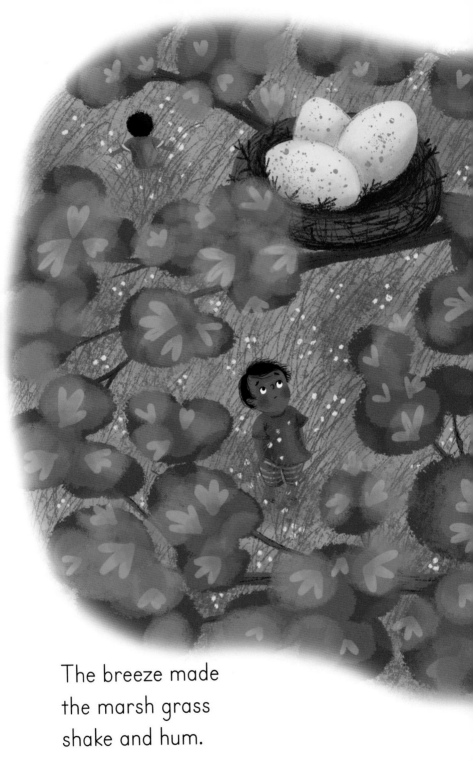

The breeze made
the marsh grass
shake and hum.

Scott looked at the
big nest on top of
the tall tree.

The key was not there, so they
went back to the creek to splash.

They saw an otter slide in the creek as they came close.

It was fun to see it swim,
twist, and play!

The otter had a clam from the mud to eat. It was hard to crack.

Scott and Jon saw the otter
use a tool to crack its clam.

Did the tool shine?

Yes, it was Dad's key!

They ran home to tell Mom. Mom said that otters use tools such as rocks and shells.

It is a smart otter! It saw Dad's key and kept it for a tool!

Dad had left to tell Mr. Brown that the car was safe in the shed but not fixed.

He came home, and the boys
said they found the key.

As the sun set, all the Gills
went to the creek.

Soon, the otter slid back into the creek. It had a clam and its smart tool.

Dad saw it use the key
as a tool, and he smiled.

38

"I need the key to get my tools, but the otter has my key for its tool," he said.

"I can get a lock at the store so the otter can keep the key. It is a smart otter."

Dad cut the lock off the shed.
The lock from the store fit fine.

He clipped his key on a
chain tied to his belt.

He kept his tools safe in the shed
and his key safe on his belt.

MORE BOOKS FROM THE GOOD AND THE BEAUTIFUL LIBRARY

I Am Molly. This Is Mac.
by Molly Sanchez

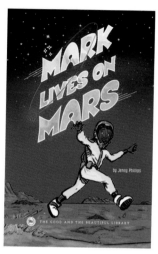

Mark Lives on Mars
by Jenny Phillips

Jack and the Lost Maze
by Jenny Phillips

Jane and the King
by Jenny Phillips